LIFE CYCLE

Poetry for the Evolving

DAMIEN THOMPSON

Revised & Updated 2nd Edition

Transitional Characters Publishing

For permissions contact: damien8thompson@gmail.com

Cover by Damien Thompson

Print ISBN: 979-8-218-72354-5

First Edition: October 2020
Second Edition: July 2025

This book is dedicated to my son

CONTENTS

BIRTHS

∞

Let the light shine soft, like our skin.
Let the brilliance take the sight from our eyes.
There is nowhere to go.

HEAVEN OR HELL

Well, I don't believe in heaven or hell
As being far away liquid places,
But last night I kissed an angel
Who whispered and giggled through my embraces.
The sun tapped me awake this morning,
Clutching my empty bed,
Chuckling softly,
Silly boy, had you never let go,
You'd have let heaven go to your head.

I'll Remember

I'll REMEMBER
ALL THAT ANYONE COULD ASK
DAY IN DAY OUT
THE THINGS YOU SAY THE WAY YOU LOOK
THE CHANGE THAT YOU BECOME

All Things Me

You are peaceful.
When I try to think about it I get anxious.
I push it to arm's length to try and study it.
It is a strength and I am a little boy awed, wondering if it could
    hurt me.
I feel stupid for feeling that way.
So I study me. Outprioritizing your peace for now.

And after a period of study, I realize where I've gone.
I look up and see you.
I see you.
I see you see me.

I imagine you standing there. Just being for the time. Studying
    me study me.
I feel warm thinking about the safety in that. The choice to, and
    the empathy with which you do.
You whisper soft and sweet to my sometimes-crying heart.

I feel as if, in this repeated process, the time of study continues
    to shrink.
I begin to recognize the inefficiency of flinching so hard at
    forward motion.
That recognition begins to weave a tapestry of risk and trust.

I see that is true of my relationship with myself, as well.
I imagine you do it too.
It seems to be a larger process, not defined by my ego.
Not defined by all things me.

THE LITTLE GIRL WHO COULD

The little girl who could
She stands so tall
Maybe loud,
Maybe proud,
She announces to me
"We're going back through"
They didn't get
Our order
Right.
She's just like a summer rain
To me
So cool
So fresh
So new
Her shadow gives her away sometimes
Not as brave
As she
Would choose
She plays among the children
Mind you
The young
The hurt
Confused.
Her heart is like an ocean
And her smile
Her smile

Commands you do.
And I'm prone to melt
When I can say out loud
Yes, I love her, too.

Like Van Gogh

The air is chill on my face
Long sleeve shirt weather
The sky is sunlit yet muddy
I smell a rich and distant fireplace

Time to harvest the leaves and leather,
Soup and bone, cold as stone
Moonlit children, tribal dance
Free falling hope, without a tether.

Standing in a field with the silence of a phone,
Amongst all the things I had yet to say,
Under shattered color wheel,
Bruised leaves fly away.

We are like Van Gogh,
Bleeding out our pain,
Swirls upon an autumn sky,
More beauty with every strain

We're a pair of sunflowers,
Yearning for the sun
Colors shining separately
Pushing into one.

The air is chill on my face
Long sleeve shirt weather
The sky is sunlit yet muddy
I smell a rich and distant fireplace

Baby Boy

If I had never met you,
I would fall apart
And with the scattered pieces
I'd ask the next passerby
To build you,
My heart

The world will try to bend you
Stand strong, but not scared to change.
Fluid like the ocean,
Return to truth
Yet never the same

And I'll be there to lend a hand
If you should ever stray
The threads that hold
The two of us,
Could never ever fray.

This Little Lion

This little lion,
Rolling in the grass,
Mewing soft and needy
Fur soft and fluffy
At play with the world.

Teeth still sharp
Roar still strong
Ready for whatever may come.

All the pieces are in place.
He doesn't doubt who or what he is,
No reason you should

Just add love and guidance,
As he fulfills his understood destiny
Growing exponentially.

He doesn't need your pride.
He brought his own.
This little lion.

In The Music Room

Entirely paneled in orange wood
With a big hi-fi stereo
And a comfortable leather chair
My father played his albums.

He played everything from Michael Jackson
Stevie Wonder, Hall & Oates
Itzhak Perlman
And the Alan Parsons Project
He knew just what record
To spin to send me
Into speaking in tongues
And dancing like a Wildman
The biggest smile plastered on my face
And when he transitioned
A deep groove was cut into the vinyl of my brain

He played a record
That wasn't danceable
That stirred in him somewhere
A teenager from the summer of love
Wrestling with adults peppered with failure and hate

Triumphs and heartbreaks
And other lifetimes swirled
In front of his eyes between us
Like some glaucoma
Wanting to take him back

He awkwardly played the air drums
In broken fits
And tried to fit back in the skin
Outside of these roles
Father and husband
Adult
And I just danced
Boy did I dance then.

Farmer's Son

I wasn't born a farmer's son
Never learned how to turn the plow
I was raised in the south of town
Only learned how to turn around

And in the thirst of a drying plain
I was twisted with different grain
Taught to lie and taught to steal
I learned to go without a meal

And you will judge me
Through a genealogy of voices
My own path that I've tread
And you will judge me
This hair that I have grown
This smile that I have shed.

I wasn't born a farmer's son.
Never learned to turn the plow

What is it to be a man
Intimate and telling,
Or hold tight while you can
Weathered implements that rust in open fields
Yearning for a duty
But unwillingness to yield.

Lost among the chaff
We ache for the sky

I wasn't born a farmer's son
Never learned how to live and die
Taught to fight and taught to run
Never learned how to settle down.

The Wild

It is the wild, which creeps in while I sit alone.
…No
it is not the wild.
It is the depth of abandonment.
It is the amount of dissonance
The mirror was willing to hold.
The greatest fissure:
In my skull.
When I desperately searched inside myself for a place to
    hide.
My life blown apart by the storm outside.
Coloring my nights in familial dark.
A muscle memory I've not logically shed.
No, it is not the wild.
The wild waits in the wings,
Intent on my permission.

ALONE(LY)

Where are you today?
Sitting alone with yourself.
The two of you so lonely.
Your twin hearts swelling in united thirst.
As you look across the water.

WE ALL WAITED

If the universe should die before me
The darkened hallway outside my bedroom should diffuse
    to full black
As I wake to alarm
If the echoing sadness of repeated arguments
Should spread its ruin of paralysis one final time
With shock and awe
Usurping the morning dew's chance to fall hesitantly an-
    other tomorrow,
The sharp intake of breath simply disappearing
In open-eyed stare
While we all waited.
We all waited.
How long did we all wait?

GYPSY

Gypsy
From moment to moment.
I swim deep into the setting suns
Looking for a new day which has yet begun.
Washing through voids without label.
Sometimes Cain. Sometimes Abel.

WE HOLD OUR OWN

Within the wind,
And fallen leaves
Amongst the frost and natural decay
A visual poem
Two great oaks grow.
Branches overlap with black and brown grooves
New buds and old stops
Entwined
Existence needs no word.
Life provides
Beautiful sustenance.

DEATHS

∞

As the last few petals fall away,
I try to save this flower of a day,
How human to want what I can't have,
I let it slip away with a tear and a laugh.

What is this Death

What is this death?
That plays around the edges of our experience.
Holding the only answers we seek
Yet keeping them in pitch dark corners of attachment

Who is this death
We carve with lore
Insulated with unknown fears
Illuminated with promise
All the better to hold you with, my dear.

Where is this death
That curves sharply in the path ahead
Shrouded by trees and ideas we've not yet formed
Lumbering along like an elephant in the room.
Brilliant and bothersome

Why is this death
If but to become next
And yet
An ambiguous invitation

What what what is this death
All around
Why do I seek to transcend it so
A grand finale

The curtain sweep.
While it diffuses through the periphery

I'm not obsessed with life in bloom
It doesn't apply to me
This is not black and white.
It is only colorless void.
Pulling and warping
Even the thought processes I feign
To parry it with
Dirty oil streaked water swirling toward the drain

Why why why do I give it so much effort so much time
Laughing it melts the ambition I loathe.
The expectations the idealizations
Object attachments and coded murky infantile needs all
    withering in their places.

Where is this death
So we can cut to the chase

DAYS LIKE THIS

We spin
So fast that we stand still.
We build and destroy
We civilize and scrutinize.
We define and redefine
importance
We spin
Tall tales and whys and hows to
live
We age
We writhe and lie and try to
stall time.
We create
We create
We create
We create new possibilities
Of why we should live
We create new hate

I spin
So fast with each new thrill
I'm all talent and no skill.
I hypothesize and accessorize.
I'm a void to be filled.

I spin

I age

I hate
I hate
I hate

I hate myself on days like this

Living, Out Loud

You can never say it out loud.
You can think it
Plan and consider
Wonder the impact
While you juggle
The seething and the seeping.
You can imagine the resilience
Compassionately
Quietly
Dial up explanations
That dissipate with slightest breath.

You can look deeply deeply deeply
Into the pool of another
Watch their repetitions.
Astrally hold them
In soulful projection,
An invisible stroke of their hair.

But you mustn't
Compel them into action.
Trigger their stalwart conditioning.
Enlist their deaf solutions.
No.
You can think it.
But you must never say it out loud.

Vacuum

This is such a vacuum,
Your voice ringing hollow,
As if my ears were broken,
You smile, deceitful insects springing to flight
And freeing themselves from your dry lips
Caked with fallacy,
I hate your plastic person,
Abhor your ignorant speak
I want to scrub my brain
Of meeting you.
Pluck my poisoned eyes from their sockets
Wash them in bleach

I'm ashamed of the energy I waste on you,
Weakening myself with disdain,
Yet you temper me with every move,

Vitality born of witlessness,
You grin and I imagine vomiting,
While throwing wild punches,
Wishing for one contact
To see your head roll.

Dreams can come true.
And my fist reaches your tallow knot

Yet I've already spun in a circle.

You've turned to smoke.

The arc of my attack still lazily framed,
In air so stale
It shows my reflection.

THE CAT IS GOD

The cat is God
And runs from my cigarette smoke.
The front porch step is hard and cold
As I stare out at the circular horizon,
The world is a bubble.
I am trapped inside myself
In a bubble.
The leafless trees genuflect,
No body is here,
Red berries cling limply to the bush
Waiting to be released.

My Father, In Mind

You aren't good enough!
My mind tells me over and over.
I beat my head against these prison bars.
Death is the filter I see through.
Everything is on its way out.
I am falling down.
I am not getting up.
This travesty and the next.
I am so sorry for myself.
That I hate myself.
Poor little baby
With the pity party.
You are not getting out.
Your temper tantrums
Of rage and dis-ease
Do not disrupt the world as you think
They rattle and shake your crib.
Making you sea-sick in the polluted ocean of your
    attachments.

Sitting in your own shit
Whining to no one.
Where is the end to this baleful torment
Imposed by me
The me that I've created
This defined martyr.
I want to kill him.

But suicide would destroy this role
Which is the one thing I refuse to do
As I do it so well.

Pus and infection in a molecular existence
Damage damage damage
You can't do it.
You are nothing.
You are a baby.
Go tell your mommy.
You fucking baby.
I refuse to show you who I am.
If you are looking for a model,
Look to my spoiled death.

The Tower and the Dancer

An arrow caught hard in the chest,
Seemed it might pass right through
So I held it there
Enduring you.
Dancing pirouettes in flowers around me
I stood a minaret, unwavering subtlety.

Grass-stained and sweating with a purple sun setting,
You smiled, and I knew you'd dance tomorrow.

But the tower cannot bend to kiss the dancer
Just echoes from my walls your calls unanswered.
That's just the way it has to be.

And on a cold and dewy morning
That came without a warning
You burst into a lemon yellow sky.
Now fatally consecrated
In dreams I hesitated
Butterflies are floating where you used to dance.

Now the moss grows up around me
And vultures they surround me
To peck the weathered concrete until it bleeds.

But the tower cannot bend to kiss the dancer
Just echoes from my walls your calls unanswered.
That's just the way it has to be.

HEAD FIRST

The music over the intercom,
The smell of books.
Tea coursing through my veins.
The conversations and the laughter
A song my wife loves
Symbolizing her freedoms…

They all rise in deafening cacophony
And I feel my body may explode, head first.
If it won't, or it doesn't
I'll do it myself.
And I do, in my mind
Sitting silently right here.
No one the wiser.
Would I be arrested? Institutionalized?
Spit on and laughed at?
If I fell apart
Melted on the floor of this well-known establishment.
A watery mess with no boundaries
Creeping brashly
But slowly
To the farthest edges of the floor.
Soaking their steps in my filth.

If I Had a Home

If I had a home
I would build a white picket fence around,
To hold our big yellow dog.
The fence, perfectly sanded, would offer no splinters.
The dog, wise and agile, would unconditionally protect us
    from harm.
The neighbors -
Oh, we would love the neighbors.
Never judging; To each his own.
There would be BBQs.
If I had a home.

BLIND

Staring straight ahead,
It seems the night goes on forever.
There are no shapes.
A sea so black, anything is there.
All that I can dream,
As my foot sidles squarely
Against a shadowed mass.
And my face peels away
Against the night's pavement.
My mind screams "You are blind!"
"You see nothing!"

TRAGIC HERO

The tragic hero's whisper
Calls from the mirror's liquid pool
Always ready for battle.
A ceaseless tear poised like the last leaf of fall.

With a cry, I turn on him.
Demanding silence,
I don my armor.
Without restraint, his voice is stereo.
With a tired fist,
I swing pacifism
But the framed glass remains intact.
My hand now clutched to my heart
In iron gauntlet
A salty tear begins to rust my chain mail.
No! I bellow as I run
Without reflection toward the battlefield.

THE YEAR YOU STOPPED LISTENING

Smiling messengers
A dose of poison.
Let us choose not to swallow!
It is too late.
From across the barren desert
I futilely throw words of warning
As you watch my soundless mouth move,
You see me screaming at you.

LITTLE PUTTY

Little putty.
That's what he was.
The stretchy and fun kind that was clean and thirsty for
    newspaper ink.
Untouched and squishy.
Anxious to be molded into some new shape.
And each night we would put the little putty back into its
    hard plastic oval container.
Protecting it from sediment. Protecting it from drying out.
Keeping stray hairs and dust, dander and coffee grounds
    from getting to it.
Keeping it pure and smooth.

Life is not simple.
And novelty fades.
We got distracted and forgot to put the little putty back in
    its container some times.
We laid it on the National Enquirer and on the shag carpet.
Pretty soon the little putty was tougher, gritty even and
    slightly smudged.
The container became less of a concern, though we tried,
And took turns molding the putty into forms we liked.
She had met someone who said he had grand ideas about
    putty and carried a list of the appropriate shapes it
    should be molded into.
He pushed and pulled our little putty.
It was not his putty.

He did not have a memory for its smooth skin, its pink
    sheen and its thirst to mold to all new shapes.
He had his own putty and ours was not the kind he liked.
He thought it low quality and underperforming to the list
    of 100 accountabilities he was tethered,
He threw it to the side, redirecting her -
The list! He cried out, afraid his silence was a waste of time.
He grew agitated and pouty with impatience.
He again looked back to the list he'd been given.
Our little putty lay still, carrying ink from the same old
    newspapers, sprouting hair and swallowing sand.
Necessity took the place of form.
Function took the place of creativity.

She studied and studied the list.
When his patience finally snapped, he struck and tore at
    our little putty, determined to make it another, as one
    determines to make wine from water.
He craved alchemy and spat out gravel. It scared him.
In secret, he counted his inkless soft spots.

Our putty naturally pulled back into itself, while attempting
    to slowly leech out the grit.
And when she brought our little putty back to me, I turned
    it over in my hands.
I tried to push his little tears back together, and looked at
    the rock and dirt stuck in various creases; saw the finger
    prints ridged over its original terrain.
Little pock marks had formed where the surface could no
    longer reconnect, and the depths showed.
Some of the sediment had simply incorporated itself.

It was still marvelous.
I was still caught by its elasticity and otherworldly nature,
 the skin still pink in spots and the way, albeit slower this
 time, its character was to pull back together.
But I hadn't forgotten, if I'd ever really remembered.

We had lost the container long ago.
He wouldn't fit in there anymore, anyhow.
Little putty.
That's what he was.

DRIFTING AWAY

You were never going to let me
I see that now.
I must stay two-dimensional
A horror without a voice

The good times and bad
Must presently fade
Too dangerous to see me as human
Capable of mistakes
Capable of change

I will always love you
Though the face will become mostly unrecognizable

WHEN YOU BECOME A DAD

You learn
What you're capable of

The role
Is all set up

You'll swell into it
With softness and pride
Naiveté and gloss

Just don't get divorced, kid
Then you'll learn
What they'll let you do

You'll thin
You'll learn
What's important
To fight for

And your child will too.

You'll be given
One handcuff and stuck in a room
With one window

They'll all pass by
Liquid glass

Shapes in flux
Older, each time

Your child will love you
Love you
(not good enough)
Love you
(not like you could love yourself)
    will look fondly
In the window
Never seeing the handcuff

Never imagining what it might be
If you were not divided
Out in the world with them.
But you will know.
Your wrist will be numb and callused
With the pulling
But you will know.

KILLING MY SELVES

I wake to silence,
The whole silence.
The silence after a great electrical discharge of thunder.
Before the rain begins.
A great tide has turned with the ripples yet to reach shore.
A mountain emerging.
The silence before a life slips away.
Or just before a new life is born.
This burgeoning reinvention.

No One Gets Out Alive

She was so young.
Unsteady
When I left her
I had to leave her

Rituals-
Dances
Garlic necklaces
False selves and
Eyes over shoulders
The rituals I had devised…

Were not enough
To protect two
The air was putrid
The time was ripe
And I had to…
I had to steal my freedom

She had been bitten
A ritual.
Rituals that had started long before.

But the piercing (screams)
Teeth gnashed and
Masticated
Crushed
When my shadow slid down the doorway

Once – letting my guard down
I'd crept back
In weakness. Just to see.
I remembered the look
Her eyes gone hollow
Staring through me
Wise to the draw
The slightest drop
Dull blood from her lip
She had begun developing her taste

I sought simple ramparts
My beard tired to gray
Running through the rituals
Over and over again.
Dancing for necessity.
I looked for no reflections
In solitude
I paled

It was quiet
Quiet and cold
When she returned

At first she didn't want much
Just a taste
To feel alive.

I gave
I gave piously

Her hollow eyes
Spun
With the rituals.
As if she'd recorded a child's mockup
Of a Shakespearean play
They unfolded for me

With me

In guileless charade

I saw myself
Again
Spinning in garlic necklace
Parading my false self
Glances tearing over shoulders

Depleted I sent her away

But the piercing (screams)
Ring of the phone
Ring ring ring!
Ring! Ring!
Rattled my insides
Trembled my brain
Stole my vision
And the knocks on the door
Bang bang bang!
Bang! Bang!
The unsophistication of death
She shrouded my doorstep
In child's outline

No! No! No!
The piercing (screams)
I slammed the door
But the skeleton of my simple shelter
Agitated with soundless entrance

And as she turned
Without curiosity
My hollow eyes followed her
Once again
Wise to the draw

Mocking the rituals and
Whispering
No one gets out alive.

Neuro Appointment

"Do you want me to stay?"

"It's up to you."

"No, it's up to you. You need to tell me."

"Well, you've got Lulu."

"Oh no, she's at home in the kennel. She's fine."

A pause.

"So, you need to tell me. Should I stay?"

"Well, you can go."

"Are you sure?"

"Yeah, that's fine."

"Okay. Well, I'll see you in a little bit then."

The lady, who appears to be either a sister or maybe even a
     daughter of the older woman walks towards the door of
     the neurology clinic. My mind whimpers, "Stay, nobody
     wants to be here alone."

It seems I can feel the woman, who is sitting right next to
     me, magnetically pulling me. At one point she reaches
     into her right pocket, which causes her to nearly lean
     into my lap.

We both need that. We are here together, even if not
     speaking.

I can't seem to find the words today to tell her.

I hate this place. I would have told her to stay.

I don't want to be here alone. I'm scared.
If I could have found the words, I would have told her.
But the window has closed.

"Paul?"

EMOTIONAL SCLEROSIS

I gave them away
My emotions
You shan't see me flinch.
Collected I stand
Numbness moving into
My fingers and hands.

I am a shadow.
No harm in being seen.
I'm losing sensation in my toes and my feet.

While ducking and dodging,
I feel a wave down my spine.
Actually I don't,
And sometimes I can't feel my stomach at all.
I still refuse to cry.

There's a clinical name, of course.
But it started with my laughter.
And I think
If I went blind,
Only the wind of my mind
Would blow
Inside this box with no edges.
The needle floating between frequency bleed.

EXTINGUISH

The red flame of anger burns
Heavier and heavier in my brain,
I run as fast as I can to keep it going because
If I slowed I would understand it
And it would extinguish.

IV Dreams

The schizophrenia of standing still.
Who are you when there is no defining choice to be made?
My fading neon sign crackles at this fleeting definition.

Death Of A Young Parent

Look at me, young man
We are but children
Begging each other's attention
Year over year
Season turning to season

Grasping delicate fingers unfastening the buttons
Of my warm parka
Loosening the knot in my tie
Pulling me to the ground without words

An incredibly shrinking man
I crawl among them
Startled by sound
Overwhelmed by color
Wide-eyed
Soft-skinned

Look at me, young man
We two are not yet equipped for this world
And its demands
My feet slide in my dress shoes
While we ritually dance

Look at me, young man
Who are we to play captain
Of this unmoored vessel

Cutting the bruised sky
In imagined direction

Let us lie
Murmuring softly together
As the winter blind
Folds in
And fades again.

REFLECTION

Reflection, today I swim in my ability to love and be loved.
The ways in which it triggers another heart,
So desperate to love and be loved.
The pain, which bubbles over and out,
Caustic, lonely and desperate.
The stories we fit over each other
Like the mask of a dead president,
Aiming to storm the vault.
The fears of letting someone in so deep
Yet desiring them with a paralyzing depth.
We cannot go any further.

Page 34

I don't want to write
Though I told myself
I would
I'm tired
Though I told myself every day.
There are ideas
Flashes of insight
Topics
The past.
They all have threads.
As I begin to pull one,
I tell myself it's not strong enough.
It's boring.
I don't see the route.
So I begin to pull another
But it's thin
It's breaking.
I don't get it.
I just don't get it.
My fingers are tired.
I deserve rest.
So I'll sleep and try again tomorrow.
Somewhere in another apartment
In another city
By dim light
Another artist dies unrealized.

REBIRTHS

∞

My eyes closed, but lo the night went on and broke anyhow.

TRANSITION

The Buddha statue sits on the table, ceramic, still and
    smiling.
The off-cream walls of the little kitchen buzz with fluores-
    cent light.
Crammed with a house worth of pots, pans and utensils.
Random Christmas decorations appear throughout
Slight rays of sunshine cut through the cheapest plastic
    blinds, broken from tenant to tenant.
Despite the outliers, there is mostly function.
Sleep in bed.
Kill time with television.
Drink coffee and stab laptop keys at kitchen table.
Heat things on stove.
Shit in toilet.
From the sounds of it, my neighbors agree.
If we were to take the walls off, we might appear a colony of
    ants or naked mole rats.
The cats don't seem to mind.
Though they sleep a lot.

REVELATION

HA.
A revelation.
There is something to this.

This feeling of weakness again
At the height of my power
Squirming in rejection
You, now my only master

But for this split second
I see it.
You without the throne

I realize the memory
Hiding from every other time

The rise to purity
The disappointing fall
They were all disasters
Something to mourn.

And here we are again
But I wonder, who is mourning?

You, as you knew you should?
Or me? Willing to fall for it again
You cannot blind me
I, only I can blind me.

LIBRARY

I go to the library
It's quiet there.
Though my mind continues to make noise.
I surround myself with the voices of all those who have gone
    before me.
All their words.
I hear none of them.
I sit in the shroud of my own sounds.
Unsure how to respond.

Photographs

These worthless photographs
They pretend
They look familiar and they act the same.
But the sand has still moved grain by grain

LIFE AND ART

Both life and art reflect truth above your hiding.
I have suffered and written sad songs.
I have allowed myself the rebirth of a sunrise and written
     songs of hope.
Lately I cannot shake an anger; I bring it in everything I do.
It is painstaking for all involved.
But I know it is necessary; part of the process. A catalyst.
There will only be so many angry songs to write
I will only attack life with this intensity for so long.
I won't understand the transition
I won't need to.
But through a gradual softening, mellowing, an ailment or
     tragedy, or perhaps a simple peace,
I will slow.
I will downshift.
I fight everyday, wrapped in the struggle,
Blindly and ignorantly
Trying to bring change ahead of itself.
There is no waiting.
Though eventually I will feel as if I waited.

THE ROAD A LOOPED RIBBON

I drop him off at school
In another city
The highway rolls ahead of me going home
There was a game...

When I was a kid
The road a plastic ribbon,
A plastic wheel and a plastic car
Pretending to navigate

An orange and purple horizon
Beautiful considering,
I think
Since we're under winter weather advisory.

I'm doing 80
When the engine begins to shake
An orange light flashes doom
My pulse pumps in cadence
Jerking
Shaking
40 miles to go
White knuckling
Please
War torn and shell shocked
I bounce in a spot at my complex.
I barely made it.
Again.

WELL?

Are you?
Or are you not?
Will you?
Or will you not?
Do you perch on the pinhead
Proud of your palisade
Do you tell them all
About your endeavors?
Do you tie up
To dress down
And give the boys
Some smart words?
Or do you shut up
Sit down
And lay it out?
Are you?
Or are you not
A writer?

Going Through A Thing

I'm going through a thing
It's just a thing
I don't need advice about the thing
There is no solving the thing
The solution is to just go through the thing
I'd tell you about the thing
But I'm afraid you'd try to see it as any more than a thing
And it's just a thing

The Chords Ring Softly In The Background

He was a high school football player
With promise
Would play college ball
For a year
Didn't know his dad
His stepdad was around
Had principles
Though drugs were involved
More than I knew
At the time

He would hug me tight
Real tight
Real love
Brothers in suffering
We spoke deeply
Truthfully
To each other
It was raw
Ancient and lovely
Though he was often on the move

I was adrift
Pieces and parts
Of role models
I liked his stepdad

He moved out of state
Right after becoming
Disenchanted
With football
I was being dumped
The mountains called
Drugs were involved
More than I knew
At the time

He would never come back

Though he would write periodically
Sometimes a random
Audio or video clip
That I would spend hours trying to decipher

It's a deep old song
I've forgotten the words to.
Though the chords ring softly in the background.

I Love You Too

Since you have the day off why don't you pick me up for lunch?
And I will. I will shelve all of the plans that I had originally made
to come get you for an hour.
You will talk incessantly about things that make little to no differ-
ence in life or death; little to no difference in regards to the path
that we're on.
And when its time to leave you'll say I love you.
And I'll say I love you too.

I'll say it for the glimpses of clarity where we talk and listen.
The moments where you show up and just hold me when I'm having
a terrible day.
Times when I'm able to actually see what you need and be of service
to you, the hard times that we both get through and squeeze each
other's hand afterwards knowing what a motherfucker that was.

I'll say it for that.
Though I know that you just want to own me.

Like everyone else you just want to put me in places
fill voids
I am a magnificent poster of Cirque du Soleil
with wispy and bleeding colors your imagination absorbs and bends
around
and you fill your empty spaces with my larger than life characters.
You want me to dance in your mind in all of my perfection and
accepted imperfections in an illusion of actually seeing me.

And when the car breaks down, you will call me.
Not because Greg knows anything about cars.
But because it feels secure to have a Greg.
It feels secure to stuff me like cotton and gauze into the open wounds that go without any further discussion.
Push me deeply,
Potentially unwilling or unwittingly
Into places where other people or objects or circumstance should have delivered;
Should have come through.

I love you too.

Ishmael

The elementary school was centralized in the eastern part of town. Home to diverse groups of students.

The volunteer reading program a way to engage with the outside world.

A way to sharpen your skills.

When called upon, your 5-year-old brow furrowed and you marched to the hallway.

A sweet face. A lived-in soul.

I asked if you preferred to read. Some kids liked me to read to them. You didn't answer. You preferred not to engage me, as if I were a nuisance to your sweet inner calm, which appeared to have been bothered enough.

You began pressing through the book. When I would smile or laugh at a page, you would stare at the page with your antenna feeling me, before navigating ahead.

The Serbian craftsman in you, the elderly carpenter, the worldly blacksmith tensed his brow at words that were a struggle; words that interrupted the natural flow of how easy things should be in Kindergarten.   Tensed again when I would attempt to help.

At the end, I smiled and exclaimed how fun the book was. You didn't look at me, but took it from me and scooted out of your chair, marching back to your duty in the classroom.

Two years later I still wonder of the whale you were pitted against. I still lightly run my fingers over my own arm, comforting us both, lamenting our difficulty, swaddling our immediate manhood.

SPECIAL

In the beginning I wanted to be special.
I wanted to reach the heights that an only child from a divorced
family was destined for.
I wanted to finally quiet the voice inside me,
So intent on discussing my worth.

And so I did.
I became special.
I looked at myself over and over again
And over again
Through the microscope of my specialness.
I felt special knowing that other people must see it too, so I pre-
tended to be humble.
Because that's what us specials do.

Soon though, the voice in me grew suspicious.
It questioned again, my worth.
The worth of being special.
What good was it?
What good could it do?
I staunchly defended its utility.

Slowly the lens slipped more and more from my eyes.
I grew older and more exposed to the wild
I weathered more storms. I lost more things.
The grains of sand steadily slipped unnoticed through my inciden-
tal hourglass.

I looked up to see special was not enough.
The cup I sought to fill would only hold enough drink for all, but not for one.
So I set my sights on connection.
It was there, holding hands and feeling the resonance of a million souls
Long dead and nascent for life
I was able to exhale.

FIGHTING IN THE PRESENT

I used to think about karate and Jeet Kune Do.

I would walk the streets late at night and plan wrist locks, Tiger uppercuts and kicking someone's knee out if necessary, to stop an attack.

Now I walk and I think, I wonder if I can look deep into this human being's soul. Deep enough to scare him into seeing life is not the game he thought it was.

Instead it is a much deeper game, where in a different time and place we might find our roles reversed.

Me holding the muzzle of the gun to his head, or my own. I must stay present enough to save us both.

Slippin' Valves

For a time I worked in an Irish Pub that served some of the best eats around.
A place of lore that lit up on any given night
With live music sing-alongs and shamrocked pints of Guinness.
There was another fella who worked there I didn't really know
He lit up to me I could tell. Like so many others he misinterpreted me as cool. The insecurities and life-pondering creating some pool of reflection to crawl into.
But I was down to get out of mind at any given time, so I agreed to go sing karaoke with him one night.
After the last note, we decided to head out and smoke a bowl. I was in good at the time.

When I got to where I wanted to be, it was time to take him home. I was in between cars again, so I was driving my stepdad's old Ford pickup he used for working around his property. He was tired of the way I drove it. Told me I had the valves slippin'.

My coworker was liquid. Slow moving with a cumulus smile. I threw on "Pali Gap" by Hendrix then got out my harmonica.
As we sailed through the colors that night back to wherever he went, I worked the clutch, the stick shift, the harmonica and a cigarette while wheeling around corners. I wasn't formally trained on the harmonica but I played every damn note to that song.

I could see in his eyes he was in the outer rims, bathing in the looking in, from outside.

Then eyeballing me like some alien. But not like I was crazy or self-destructive.

He recognized that somehow in that ride back I'd harnessed it. I realized it too. It was Aikido, rolling with every change. Zen wasn't always sober. I just laughed. I was just down to get out of my mind at any given time.

THE SPACES IN BETWEEN

Overall, I'm not doing too bad, I think
Surveying the interior of my apartment.
There are clothes that need put away.
There are recyclables piling which have not been recycled.
We have no couch but there are chairs.
A stray Christmas ornament or two may see Valentine's Day
Mail. Mail is a problem.
The exterior space seemingly a reflection of the inner space.
But my surfaces are mostly clean.

My father's house post-divorce was less exculpatory,
walled in with comics, albums, books, and dust.
Pornography and overflowing ashtrays.
Somehow food
had gotten on the kitchen ceiling a long time ago,
likely from one of the dishes flowing out of the sink and over the
counter.
The rabbit cage sitting in the middle of the living room floor was
a movie theater popcorn machine, pillowing feces onto the floor.
The rabbit "went crazy" later that year and disappeared.

The air was thick.
Not just with cigarette smoke and cheap incense from time to time.
It was thick with stunted exhale.
Clogged pores.
Sleepless nights and thoughts unsaid.
Static electricity that turned to static.

As We Awaken

We were laying on the floor talking and laughing
There was a movie playing in the background
He got giggly and silly talking in made up voices
"I'm weird. Around you anyways."
I smiled. "Oh yeah?"
"Yeah I'm not like this around my friends, or my mom."

Not thinking much of my reply, I asked "Are you hiding?"
He started laughing more
To belie the kernel of truth I may have polished a corner of,
"No, I don't think so."
 Shook his head.
"Only you."
"Only you would ask something so deep with a little smile."
He grinned wide pondering this whole interaction.

I smiled and felt tears behind my eyes.
It's not my reliance on his importance or his validation, though I
don't deny its existence.
It's the rift. Bordered by highways and humans. The natural pro-
gression into independence prickled with unnatural dramas and
unnatural players.
It's the glimpses of health and thinking. Emotional awareness and
maturity.
It's the healing and the nights I can sleep after witnessing his
resilience.
Okay. Okay. Okay.

On Your Anniversary

I hear you scratching
Though I try to ignore
The air begins to waft with the slightest flume
I hear Virgil's voice beginning to point out the flames
Crossing over into your neighborhood
So many words and catchphrases
Expressions and behaviors
So few of which matched what you were actually saying.
Puzzles for me to solve.
Traps for me to avoid.
Perhaps looking for the validation I can give you now.

Yes. I hear you scratching.
Your time has come.
Again.
Though it floats in under mask.
Drives parallel to me on an adjacent highway looking over
    from time to time
The taut medicated skin of an apple riding the counter
With a silent worm pulping through brown mush just
    below.

My mother says we do not move through grief
Rather grief moves through us

You always wore a watch.
I don't, but I know what time it is.

Janus

My mother had used some of her measly print shop salary
When I was a kid
To buy mutual funds
Through a company called
Janus.
A Roman God with two faces.
God of duality.

She talked about them from time to time.
Watching them like hounds at the dog track
Betting on a brighter future
Budgeting just enough so she could also pay our mortgage

My father put stock in other things:
A good joke
A pack of smokes.
The brilliance of a rock opera or a great film.
He was on the phone constantly
Socializing or setting up gigs for his band.
He was always home with me growing up.
Called me buddy.

My mother is healthy.
The stocks never did much.
He's been dead five years.
I'm forty.

I live for my son.
Twice a week I drive to the city
His mother moved to.
I cheer him on.
Help with homework
Feed him.
Call him buddy.

When I get back home, I wonder
About the twenty-hour drive
To the coast
On a pitch dark night
And how far out I'd have to get
Before the ocean's great swaddling arms
Would lull me into sleep.

After he died the first time
Or had the massive stroke,
Dead in so many words
My mother told me he'd been a thief.
All his life.
Cigarettes, movies, comic books
Two basements full that I'd had to unload after the fact.
And he'd cheated on her.
Which seemed to crush something more
For me than her.
Something I just can't reconcile
Looking to the past.
Looking to the future.

I climb into my car

And begin the long drive to see my boy
Smile and cheer him on.
Guide him from some lovely innate place
The waves breathing and bubbling
In the rear of my mind.

SOME CRY OUT, SOME CRY IN

First, they give me the anti-inflammatory
Then, the anti-histamine.
They take a couple vials of blood
Then, they give me a steroid.

After the steroid, they unclasp
And hook up the grand finale
The drug that barters with my body
To stop destroying itself.

The fluorescents hum above me
Making everything look like a sitcom
The cabinets are faux grain
The colors drab and the wallpaper
Bleeds a color pattern that you've seen
A thousand other trips before
In a thousand other facilities
With a thousand other young women
Holding a magical secret of turning
Their hearts off when it's time to go.
It's a weird little world.

The rooms are thin and close.
Without ever seeing their faces,
I learn their most intimate details.
Hear their canned laughter
They speak loosely and without concern

I scratch away at my notebook,
Trying to transfuse my experience to paper.

Before my eyelids puff
The channel goes fuzzy
And the drab faux grains fade to a dull orange.
Letting the pages slip to my weird little world
No one the wiser.

Cooking Together

We are cooking together
Soup.
His idea
When I suggested he be in charge
Of two meals this weekend.

He's creative.
Good with a recipe.
Though he's not sure yet
When I say so.

We both have head colds.
Zombie-like
We shuffle around the kitchen
Barely thinking.
No need for words.
We know.
We feel our way.
With each other.

And I feel my heart
Slowed down.
Sick or not.
For the first time in weeks.

I'll Just Close My Eyes

I'll just close my eyes
I just wanna close my eyes
I'm just gonna close my eyes
Let the world go by
There are boulders to push and fires to tend
Demons to out and spirits to mend,
But I just wanna close my eyes.
Tomorrow.
There is always tomorrow
And I will step fresh
Tomorrow.
With fire in my breath.
I'm just gonna close my eyes.

Dancing Photons

Every thing
Air Light   Wind
Is   Some   Thing
I walk through   air
I am moved by   wind
I bask in   light
Dancing photons
My perception
The only intangible
I shake   imperceptibly

Mind's Road

My mind is like this road.
Sometimes I drive the path
Straight and smooth.
Sometimes it is bumpy
Winding through narrow curves
With limited visibility.
Occasionally I turn.
Sometimes I don't drive.
Sometimes debris on the roadside invites my perusal.
Leave the trash there.

BIRTHDAY

Here it comes again.
Another revolution you might say.
It feels like it.
Like I'm revolting against all I know.
No need for cake to tell me so.

I hear the academics:
Releasing attachments.
Resolving infancy.
Maturation.
Creating grandiose dreams that never come to fruition.
Flittering around in adolescence.
Regression in the service of development.

Do I really have time for that?
I agree with Einstein.
The most incomprehensible thing about my life, is that it is
    comprehensible.
Thereby making it all the more painful.
So must we have cake?
To celebrate?

SOMEONE ELSE'S TEARS

With distraught faces
And tear-filled eyes
They plead with me,
Do not cry.

Don't be sad
Tomorrow is a new day.

They are right.
So tomorrow is…

Lift your head
And don't worry
This sadness doesn't define you

They are wrong,
At this moment it does define me

And I know something they don't.
If you are never sad
Your happiness shall be tinged
with

Distraught faces
And tear-filled eyes,
Your mouth pleading
Do not cry
So that someone else's tears
Won't tip your cup.

FROM EDEN

Last night the devil stopped by my house pret-a-porter. It was very late. She was away from her fiancé because they'd had a fight. She looked healthier and more confident; sexier, more tempting.

She confessed she had to spend time with me and tell me that she loved me and I was special. She spoke of common interests and evoked passion in me.

Repeating a question of what I'd really been doing, she snorted and giggled at meditation and my talks of peace. She invited me to drink the alcohol she had brought. I admitted I felt thirsty.

We laughed breathlessly. But I did not drink her alcohol, even when she referred to its "naked deliciousness," or teased my wounded little boy that no girls would like him sober. My teenager did not return her playful pat on my leg. And my lion would not be blinded to the incessantly ringing phone in her pocket; gentle screams of the portal where she came from begging with gravity for her return.

Next the devil begged me to sing his favorite song, From Eden. I suggested we listen to it together, and got an apple from my kitchen.

He once again invited me for a drink. Instead I picked up my guitar and I played the devil my songs. He smiled and cooed compliments to me, sliding patiently closer. I let my soul pour out into the room and over the devil. Finally, he looked at me, gradually distant and aware of the time. I smiled.

He said he must be going, but he loved me. He coiled me into a hug and kissed me on the neck. For a moment I disconnectedly tried to hold an illusion of a past that never existed.

Then my embrace became strong with the present and I lovingly held him and his plight. I breathed the devil out and watched him slither across my lawn. A smoky silhouette under the streetlight, fractured through the prism of glass in my front door.

PATHOS

We all do it, don't we?
Our lives splashing back and forth
With ambition and expectation
Disappointment.
Like some jostled plastic ship
In a poorly sealed polyurethane toy
With distilled water and blue dye.
We shake and shiver; plan and stumble.

The Quran and the Bible tell us
We may have ambition
But we have no control; no worries.
Allah is over all things competent.
Many are the plans in the mind of man
But it is the purpose of the Lord that will stand

We all do it, don't we?
Squeeze tightly to another
With lilted words and lush routine
Holding human shield
To unconsciously deflect the unrelenting dark.

We all do it, don't we?
Greedily fill our hears and our minds
With a smart word or sparking eye.
To carry another mile before our buckets dry
With the wind of experience

The shadows lengthen as we see the unknown
Laying quietly in the minds of the assured.
Looking again; you can see
There's not that far to go.

We all do it, don't we?
Produce
Capitalize
Philosophize
Drink for a martyr
Judge
Justify
Tell lies.
Pull the shades and hide.

We all do it don't we?
And in that regard,
I don't feel so bad.

INSIDE THE VOID

Her little eyes
Poked through the dark at me
Prone for the evening
Hoping sleep would take us away

Am I just a distraction for you
Something to fill the void?
She barely asked
Bravely audible

What would I need distracting from?
I moved closer to her

Missing your son
The pain you carry all the time

I smoothed her hair
I have found distractions
Even when I wouldn't admit it
But I knew it every time
I had to
Know them
So I could recognize you.

A piece of my heart
Is missing and
With the lack of blood flow

I am cold
Much colder
When we're apart
You are a warm blanket
Wrapping me in love
Laughter
You are no distraction

She moved closer to me
I held her tight in the void
For a long quiet moment

"And I miss my son."

Nothing Unique in This

The earth spins and I change seasons. A mass of atoms wanting to believe that I mean something. The power to think about it, and realize I need something. Pitying myself while others without words make sand castles and crown kings.

We want to believe tooth for a tooth and eye for an eye. Egos aflame and sensibilities high. But really this is all about an I for a guy. Remember - the thinking. Therefore I am I. An evolutionary strength over amoebas and flies.

This life manifests from our greatest strengths and our greatest weaknesses. Row row row down the stream of this. My father wanted to believe no one else had it as unique as his. He called from his corner until no voice was as weak as his. Missing the point that there was nothing unique in this.

A friend says maybe no one wants to think as deep as this. I go back to my corner and ponder all my weaknesses. The world changes shape and I walk the streets featureless. Invisibility: a cloak to protect my ego - as if it is what I think it is.

The earth spins. I change seasons. My heart open. Love warming my reason. It is naïve and sees me without concern. I dance in the friction hoping to learn. Until smoky ribbons engulf me. A magnifying glass of vulnerability starting me to burn. I wave it away to try and clear the air. My mind churns. I head to the corner. I know it's safe there. I call out to remind love and myself of the where. I call out louder, keeping myself scared.

Back in the corner thinking of dad. Bottling tornados with words like "sad." He surrounded himself with dancing cigarette smoke to reminisce. Love just a little too close despite a silent wish. Again missing the point there was nothing unique in this.

I laugh at myself. An ego wanting another ego to behave. All my life having been a slave. Comfortable being powerless in lieu of the façade. I beat myself with grandfather's flog. Imagining shackles when freedom is a choice. I mourn to the crowd to hear my dad's voice.

The earth spins. I change seasons. Looking in the mirror of another's love helping me to think through it. Seeing love in myself the key to bliss. Life manifesting out of my greatest strengths and greatest weaknesses. I grieve and dance and aim to breathe through this.

As It Were. As It Is.

A great thermal wind
Has blown in
A sucking cavern
Pulls itself together
Where the meteor hit.
Life
As it were
Had to undo
Its tendril hold
Its harmony.
Decay must.
And now
New shoots begin
To creep their thirsty tendrils
For a new foothold.

FAINT AT HEART

We didn't know each other really.
Four years ago.
We began to get sober
Parallel paths.

We were both musicians.
Though he much more successful than I.
He was kind. Gentle. Thoughtful.
I liked what he had to say.
It came from a genuine
Hard-lived place.

We held hands a time or two.
In prayer. In hope.
Blind to our paths but seeing for the first time
A possibility. One of infinite.

We spoke of music.
Exchanged numbers
Talked of getting together
Though he wasn't driving at the time.

I read the news yesterday.
Sitting on a lake patio
Drinking iced tea.

Our paths had diverged a year or better before
But I held him on the fringe of my mind
Thinking maybe just once
I would come around
Do more than talk
About getting together.

The old searing
Was back
Seeing his soft curiously smiling face
In the major music publications.
It felt like a night
Of drinking hard whiskey
A pack of cigarettes
A short sleep.

We could swim across this lake together.
If you wanted to.
The water is beautiful.
The sun so bright.
We needn't think about the depths below.
If you become tired
Let your body go slack
And just float.

Tranquility

Tranquility
A mesmerizing tourquoise sea
Enveloping me
Ripples come and ripples go,
To trip and trickle but never slow.

SON

My son
I love you more than all
You have taught me how
I obsess over you
The innocent child I could not save
I stretch it over you.
I cry and thrash as my projector
Flickers across your face.
My conditioned response to your freedom:
Communism.
As I flog myself at the sight of my father
I suck my thumb hoping you would want to be like me.
Though I am wiser now.
I have plowed much self.
I did that for me. Though I did that for you.
We are getting older now.
Invincibility and mortality, hand in hand
I wish I saw you more
It keeps me up at night
I wish you would like to be like me
The only ego I know and love,
And then I realize I hope you choose
To be like you.
To love you more than all.
As authenticity transforms into compassion.

The Weaver

Into the wind,
The evening sought
Ne'er impeded with a thought.
To do unto
Indeed, to undo
To be all
To be none.

So, in the image,
I cast my web
Ever only to catch the ebb
But let it go
Let it go

Jump the rocks
To turn the flow
Spinning spinning spinning
Even the clever fox

So in I dove.
To turn the flow
To jump the rocks
And so on
And so on
And so on

ABOUT THE AUTHOR

Damien Thompson is a writer and musician originally from the Midwest. His literary work—short stories and poetry—has appeared in both print and online publications, including Exquisite Corpse (Vol. XIV), In Our Own Words (Vol. IV), The Stardust Review, The Hare's Paw Review, and the WILDSounds Writing Festival Anthology.

As a musician, he has released four full-length albums and numerous singles, showcasing a diverse creative voice across genres. In 2025, he published his memoir, ...And Then I Would Fly, a candid and powerful account of his turbulent childhood marked by abuse and the complex relationship with his father. The memoir was a June 2025 winner of the Literary Titan Gold Book Award.

In addition to his artistic pursuits, Thompson spent over a decade managing a national 911 call center. He later earned a Bachelor of Science in Business and is currently completing a Master of Science in Clinical Mental Health Counseling to establish a private psychotherapy practice.

www.ingramcontent.com/pod-product-compliance
Lightning Source LLC
LaVergne TN
LVHW051602080426
835510LV00020B/3101